Candletown
Can you find Puddle Lane?

USING THIS BOOK

*One of the best ways of helping children to learn to read is by reading stories to them and with them. This way they learn what **reading** is, and they will gradually come to recognise many words, and begin to read for themselves.*

First, grown-ups read the story on the left-hand pages aloud to the child.

You can reread the story as often as the child enjoys hearing it. Talk about the pictures as you go.

Later the child is encouraged to read the words under the pictures on the right-hand page.

The pages at the back of the book will give you some ideas for helping your child to read.

British Library Cataloguing in Publication Data
McCullagh, Sheila K.
　　Jeremy's ride. —(Puddle Lane series; no. 855).
　　1. Readers—1950-
　　I. Title　　II. Dillow, John　　III. Series
　　428.6　　PE1119
　　ISBN 0-7214-1052-9

First edition

Published by Ladybird Books Ltd Loughborough Leicestershire UK
Ladybird Books Inc Lewiston Maine 04240 USA

Printed in England

Jeremy's ride

written by SHEILA McCULLAGH
illustrated by JOHN DILLOW

This book belongs to:

Ladybird Books

It was Friday evening, and
the Wideawake Mice
were in Candletown market.
"It's getting dark,"
said Grandfather Mouse.
"We must go home."

"Let me just finish this nut,"
said Jeremy.

"You start off, and we'll follow,"
said Chestnut.
He had just found another nut, too,
and he didn't want to leave it.
"Well, don't be long,"
said Grandfather Mouse.
He led the way across the square.

"We must go home," said Grandfather Mouse.

"We can run much faster
than Uncle Maximus," said Jeremy.

"Yes, but we mustn't be long,"
said Chestnut. "Tom Cat
comes out in the evening."
Jeremy choked on his last piece of nut.

"All right," he said,
when he had recovered his breath.
"Let's go."

"Let's go,"
said Jeremy.

They had almost reached
the entrance to Puddle Lane,
when Chestnut stopped.
His whiskers twitched.
"There's someone about," he said.
Tom Cat sprang out of the shadows,
and leapt towards them.
"Run!" cried Chestnut,
rushing off to one side.
"Run for your life!"

"Run!" cried Chestnut.

Jeremy raced towards Puddle Lane.
Tom Cat stopped for a second.
He wasn't sure which mouse to follow.
Then he sprang after Jeremy.
The second's pause had given Jeremy
just time to reach the archway
that led to Puddle Lane.
If he had tried to run through it,
Tom Cat would have caught him.
But he didn't.
He ran up the wall of the archway
as fast as he could.

Jeremy ran
up the wall.

Tom Cat leapt up after him,
but Jeremy was just out of reach.
Tom Cat fell back to the ground.

Jeremy scrambled up the old wall,
clinging to the cracks
between the stones,
until he came to the windowsill.
He looked down.
Tom Cat was standing there,
watching him, and
slowly twitching his tail
from side to side.

Jeremy looked down.

"That was a near thing,"
said a squeaky little voice
in his ear.
Jeremy jumped round, and saw
a little mouse looking out of a hole
between two stones.
"You'd better come inside,"
said the mouse.
"I know Tom Cat. He'll just
sit there and wait for you."
Jeremy looked down.
Tom Cat was sitting
on the stones below, looking up.

Jeremy looked down.

Jeremy shivered, and
followed the mouse through the hole.
He found himself in the room
over the archway leading to Puddle Lane.
The room was empty, and
there were cobwebs on the windows.
"I'm Whiskers," said the mouse,
as soon as Jeremy was safely inside.
"I live here."

"I thought mice were called
after the names of trees," said Jeremy.

"**Wood** mice have names like that,"
said Whiskers. "I'm a house mouse.
I have a proper mouse name,
and a proper house to live in.
I don't live outside in the rain."

"I'm Whiskers,"
said the mouse.

"I live in the Magician's garden,"
said Jeremy, "and I've got to get home."

"I should stay here till morning,
if I were you," said Whiskers.
"If you go now,
Tom Cat will be waiting for you."

"But if I'm not home soon,
Grandfather will come to look for me,"
said Jeremy. "And Tom Cat
will see him. Grandfather
would never get away from Tom Cat.
He can't run fast enough."
Whiskers ran up the wall
on the far side of the room, and
looked out of another window,
up Puddle Lane.

Whiskers ran
up the wall.

"Just come and have a look," he said.
Jeremy ran across the room, and
climbed up beside him.
"What did I tell you?" said Whiskers.
"Tom Cat's there, waiting."
Jeremy looked down.
Tom Cat had come through the archway,
and was watching him
from inside Puddle Lane.

Jeremy looked down.

"But I've **got** to get home,"
said Jeremy.

"There's one way you might manage it,"
said Whiskers. "That is,
if you're not too frightened."

"What's that?" asked Jeremy.

"I saw the Magician go into the square,
a little while ago," said Whiskers.
"He'll come home this way soon.
You could jump down on his hat,
as he comes through the archway,
and get a ride home.
He'd never notice you."

"I have got
to get home,"
said Jeremy.

"I'll try," said Jeremy.

"You've got to do more
than just try," said Whiskers.
"If you miss, you'll land
on the ground, and
Tom Cat will get you."
Jeremy shivered.
"I – I think I can do it," he said.
Grandfather will be coming soon."

"This way, then," said Whiskers.
He led the way to a little hole
between two stones.

Whiskers led the way
to a little hole.

The two mice crept through the hole,
and out on to the windowsill.
The moon was shining down,
and Jeremy could see Tom Cat,
watching them from the stones below.
"Listen!" said Whiskers.
"Here's the Magician."
Jeremy heard slow footsteps
coming over the stones.
He felt almost too frightened
to move.

Jeremy saw
Tom Cat.

He looked down, and saw
the Magician's flat hat below him.
"Now!" squeaked Whiskers. "Jump!"
Jeremy jumped.
He felt himself falling through the air,
and for one dreadful moment
he thought that he had missed.

Jeremy jumped.

Then his feet landed
on the Magician's hat, and
he held on with all his claws.
His heart was beating so loudly
that it sounded like a drum
banging in his ears.

Jeremy landed on
the Magician's hat.

When he had recovered a little,
he looked around him.
He was going down Puddle Lane
at a steady pace,
on the Magician's head.
He looked back.
The lights in the houses
shone through the windows,
and he could see quite well.
Tom Cat was creeping after them,
in the shadows
at the side of the lane.
His eyes were on Jeremy.

Jeremy looked back.

Jeremy wasn't cold, but
he found himself shivering.
They came to the gates
of the Magician's garden.
As the Magician turned
to shut the gate,
he saw Tom Cat.
"Shoo! Scat! Be off with you!"
cried the Magician.

The Magician
saw Tom Cat.

Tom Cat stopped.
"Scat!" cried the Magician again.
He snapped his fingers.
A little ball of fire
fell into the lane
just in front of Tom Cat.
Tom Cat turned and fled.
He ran back down the lane
as fast as he could run,
with the little ball of fire
chasing after him.

Tom Cat ran back
down the lane.

The Magician laughed, and
snapped his fingers again.
The ball of fire disappeared.
Jeremy didn't wait.
As quick as a flash,
he jumped on to the gate, and
ran down the gate to the garden.

Jeremy ran
down the gate.

As he got to the hollow tree,
he met Grandfather Mouse.
"Jeremy!" cried Grandfather.
"I'm so glad to see you.
Chestnut came home without you.
He came home the back way.
I was just coming
to see where you were."

"I'm so glad to be home,"
said Jeremy, still shivering.
"I've had **such** an adventure."

"Come inside and tell us
all about it," said Grandfather.
"You're quite safe now."
And he followed Jeremy into the hole
under the hollow tree.

Jeremy met
Grandfather Mouse.

Notes for the parent/teacher

When you have read the story, go back to the beginning. Look at each picture and talk about it, pointing to the caption below, and reading it aloud yourself.

Run your finger along under the words as you read, so that the child learns that reading goes from left to right. (You needn't say this in so many words. Children learn many useful things about reading by just reading with you, and it is often better to let them learn by experience, rather than by explanation.) When you next go through the book, encourage the child to read the words and sentences under the illustrations.

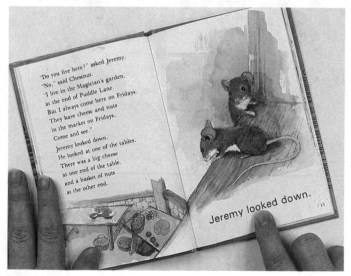

Jeremy looked down.

Don't rush in with the word before he* has time to think, but don't leave him struggling for too long. Always encourage him to feel that he is reading successfully, praising him when he does well, and avoiding criticism.

Now turn back to the beginning, and print the child's name in the space on the title page, using ordinary, not capital letters. Let him watch you print it: this is another useful experience.

*Children enjoy hearing the same story many times. Read this one as often as the child likes hearing it. The more opportunities he has of looking at the illustrations and **reading** the captions with you, the more he will come to recognise the words. Don't worry if he **remembers** rather than **reads** the captions. This is a normal stage in learning.*

If you have a number of books, let him choose which story he would like to have again.

---

*Footnote: In order to avoid the continual "she or he", "her or him", the child is referred to in this book as "he". However, the stories are equally appropriate for girls and boys.

*All the books at each Stage are separate stories
and are written at the same reading level.*

*Children should read as many books as possible
at each Stage before going on to the next Stage.*

*Have you read these other stories from Stage 1
about the mice?*

Stage 1

*from The
Wideawake Mice
find a new home*